The Book of Shi-Ji 2
Peter Maxwell Slattery

The Book of Shi-Ji 2

THE BOOK OF SHI-JI 2

Copyright © 2019 by Peter Maxwell Slattery

2nd Edition

Cover by Kesara (Christine Dennett), www.kesara.org

Editor: Jessica Bryan, www.oregoneditor.com

DISCLAIMER: The information in this book is intended to be of a general educational nature, and does not constitute medical, legal, or other professional advice for any specific individual or situation.

No part of this book may be reproduced or transmitted in any form or by any means, without permission in writing from the publisher.

Published by Peter Maxwell Slattery
Email: petermaxwellslattery@outlook.com.au
www.petermaxwellslattery.com

ISBN 978-0-244-77423-3

The Book of Shi-Ji 2

The Book of Shi-Ji 2

This book is dedicated to all Beings throughout all planes and in between, throughout the universe and beyond.

The Book of Shi-Ji 2

Peter's work in the field of UFOlogy is paramount and has the highest integrity. His courage and tenacity are reflected in his work. His ability to connect with higher dimensional beings, and film and document them, is unsurpassed.

James Gilliland
www.eceti.org
www.bbsradio.com

The Book of Shi-Ji 2

Thank you

A big thank you goes out to my family, friends, and to all my supporters and fellow Beings from the many realms in this universe and beyond for their love and support and I also thank Shi-Ji.

Love, light, and bliss,
Peter Maxwell Slattery

The Book of Shi-Ji 2

CONTENTS

Introduction..13

Chapter 1: The Elohim and You........................17

Chapter 2: The First Humans in Lyra...............33

Chapter 3: Manifesting Your Tomorrow............53

Chapter 4: Humanity's Future...........................71

Chapter 5: Assistance and Protection...............87

Chapter 6: Ascension, Energy Waves, and Opportunities...105

Chapter 7: From the Light Blueprint..............121

Chapter 8: God's Mind, Your Mind..................135

Final Note..151

Glossary..153

Books by Peter Maxwell Slattery.....................171

About the Author..173

The Book of Shi-Ji 2

INTRODUCTION

As we continue on from *The Book of Shi-Ji*, which was written by Shi-Ji through me, the information goes deeper and more wonderful and amazing. Although presented quite simply, it's complicated in a convoluted way. In Book 2, Shi-Ji expands our understanding of who we are as humans and our nature: past, present, future, and beyond, and our experiences with the many beautiful Beings who are assisting us at this time.

After the experiences that led to the writing of Shi-Ji's first book, more came to light for me, and I learned there are many facets to Shi-Ji. Now I understand she is an Elohim Being, and she has a human facet, a Light Being facet, and many other facets—not to mention (which blew my mind), the facet known as Peter Maxwell Slattery, me!

Known as a Light Being from the Star Merope in the Pleiades, Shi-Ji discusses in a multidimensional way the true and beautiful nature of human existence in this new book. Also included are messages from many other Beings who are in service to the collective.

Please note that throughout the book, Shi-Ji uses the word "here" to refer to Earth. A Glossary for some of the words that might be unfamiliar to some readers has been included.

To fully understand Shi-Ji and her messages, it is recommended that you first read *The Book of Shi-Ji*. Then you will understand how the second book brings in much more of Source's energy, and how the first book paved the way to bring in the next level of consciousness for the reader. This increase of in-depth information, concepts, and revelations are here to help the reader empower their own self, their own God self, and help them connect to that which they already know, but might have forgotten. Make of this what you may and enjoy.

Cheers!
Peter Maxwell Slattery

The Book of Shi-Ji 2

Chapter 1
The Elohim and You

You are multidimensional Beings who are having multidimensional experiences. You are a cell, a facet of Source (with many other facets), and you coexist at the same time throughout many planes. To understand this, you need to go from linear mind to multidimensional mind.

Many experiences are happening for your oversoul at this (what you call) time. So…it's best we start with the "creation through thought" story first, and then take it from there.

During the implosion and then the explosion (which created a torsion field), and then the second explosion, Helper Beings and zillions of spirits were created. They went out to experience and gain knowledge—although some remained in a state of monitoring for the overall collective, Source. This is how everything began in this cell, which is our multilayered universe, with its planes and dimensions and inter-planes.

The other universes were created this way, too. All universes have a symbiotic relationship with each other, and all together they make up a greater intelligence. When the explosion happened and the zillions of spirits and Helper Beings went out to experience and gain knowledge, there were the Elohim, who came into existence through thought.

The Elohim are the children of Source and the Higher Self, which is the oversoul with many facets. We are the Elohim! The Elohim are our direct connection to Source, the "telephone exchange" that connects our calls to whatever we are trying to reach through our intentions.

The Elohim are the regulators and gatekeepers of the paradise realms. They allow those with a higher state of consciousness, who are coming from a place of love, (which is the key) to have access to them.

The Elohim (as you) created the many light blueprints throughout this entire cell of Source and the system serving Source and the overall collective. Using these blueprints, the Elohim also created thought forms and humans, as well as many other Beings throughout the many realms.

The Elohim created the first humans by falling from the light blueprint, similar to the way a cell divides. Originally, there was only the Elohim state of vibration. From there—through thought and consciousness—another light body came from the Elohim Beings and they manifested a physical body in this reality. It was neither male nor female.

The first humans evolved in Lyra, in the Milky Way Galaxy. This has and is happening throughout all of the galaxies that are at a certain level of development. The first humans went out from Lyra and throughout the galaxy, and beyond. Eventually, they came to settle in our solar system on the planets Melona/Maldek, Mars, and Earth. The Elohim created the human experience.

The Elohim transfer knowledge from their Merkabah to your Merkabah. This is what happens when you communicate with other facets of yourself or other Beings, at least some of the time.

The Elohim make use of your Third Eye and what you call the Angelic Beings, in order to communicate and do the work of Source. They control the spectrums of light—which are very important for evolution—through the Eye of Source. This helps humans ascend back to a Being of Light and reconnect to the ascension vibration, which encompasses and has access to all vibrations.

Humans are amazing, and when they recognize the God within (recognize their mind is God's mind) they can be incredibly creative.

They can project themselves energetically out through their Third Eye in order to communicate, show imagery, or bi-locate and connect with whatever they have set their intention on.

Through the Third Eye, the human can project itself in Light Body form and manifest in the other realms and heavens—not just in light form but in any form—once they have mastered their true nature.

The Elohim (which is also you) regulate whatever you download for your experience here. Light codes, letters, and sounds are some of the keys. The Elohim created these keys and they work on multiple levels. The information from them is continually unraveling for those who see them ethereally, or in the mind's eye. Light codes, letters, and sounds can also change chemical reactions in the human and the conscious grid using energy. When humans understand this, they will understand they are like cells on the hands of Source, who work with all linear and non-intelligences.

The Elohim connect your brain to that which records everything, and they also connect you to the Astral Mansions. They can connect you to the star clusters and branches of the Star Nations, and they have a symbiotic relationship with Source. They regulate this program and all experiences within this cell of Source.

The pyramid crystal grids help amplify a certain vibration in this and other environments, which enables the Elohim to bring imagery and downloads into facets of themselves. This has been done because of the Archons (the Lower Light), the Beings that fell (as described in *The Book of Shi-Ji*).

From Source's throne and the Beings there, to the Elohim, all are in sync and govern all templates. The Elohim control and regulate the sub-cells and the beginning and end of conscious awareness. There are Beings above the Elohim and below. The Elohim regulate all and connect all.

Once everything is done (or at any time), everything can be reset when all at the collective level have made a decision to do it. The Elohim control the light blueprint from Source through God's Eye.

The Elohim continuously oversee creation through Source's Eye. They're the "Watchers" who observe the Brotherhoods of Light and everything they have created in the heavens.

Specific human forms and many other forms have been (and can be) created through the Elohim, the Third Eye, and Source. When the Elohim align Source's Eye and the humans' Third Eye, physical embodiments of the oversoul and body of light can regenerate the physical body.

When all this started, there was no need for physical procreation, because the human body was created from the Elohim realm through thought.

It wasn't until those who fell and lost connection to Source, that sex, shorter life spans, disease, and many other human experiences came into existence. Through this, creation of an Artificial Intelligence was created to work multidimensionally and hold a vibrational trap for those who fell, so they could control and, in effect, thrive and become Gods.

Those who were completely lost became slaves, after being led astray and losing their connection to Source because of what seemed like a vibrational block. Later, those who were able came back and changed the vibrational state of the lost ones and helped them reawaken to God at the unconscious and conscious levels. These are the times you are in now.

There are many Beings that came into existence on many levels from Source and the Elohim. The Being you call Archangel Metatron is one of them.

Metatron was manifested from Source in the Elohim state and created the electron for our light vehicle (the Merkabah) and for our immediate universe. Through the electron, the Elohim are connected at all times, just as everything throughout the physical and nonphysical universe is.

Archangel Michael is another Being who came into existence on many levels. He is the protector who works in sync with the Elohim and the Archangels Gabriel, Uriel, and Raphael, and a huge host of other Beings called by many different names from many different realms.

These names are actually vibrational tones, sounds, and keys to connect to them. Although the Angelic Beings depicted in your ancient scripts have been altered (over time) by manipulation, there is some truth in them.

The Guardian Beings, the Brotherhoods, the Councils, and the regulators have many names and descriptions. Some of these Beings have facets of themselves incarnated into lives here and elsewhere throughout many planes. Even now, they walk among you and visit you.

All these Beings are messengers from Source and they are your Guides. They can communicate with many of you at the same time because they are multidimensional. You are, too, and you can communicate multidimensionally.

Your unexplained mysteries have been shaped and created on a light blueprint level by the Elohim. The main program from the Divine is shaped, created, and given from the worlds of the Elohim.

Before we go any further, it would be best to explain how reincarnation does, and does not exist at the same time.

The easiest way to describe it would be to use this analogy: Imagine your oversoul, your Elohim self, as the head of an octopus, and all the lives you are experiencing (at the same time) are through the tentacles of the Octopus. At times, the experience through one tentacle might end and evolve into another experience, or it might shoot off to create a new head and more facets, in effect, creating another Octopus.

If you understand this, you will understand that you don't go from life to life. You are experiencing many lives at once! Past, present, and future are all happening and accessible at the same time.

Although you are having this Earth experience, you can access back up the tentacle to the oversoul and communicate or tap into the other lives you are also experiencing. Because the oversoul is a cell of all that is, you can tap into other cells, oversouls, experiences, knowledge, and the past, present, or future, because all is in symbiotic relationship.

Everything comes from the light blueprint and is holographic in nature. It comes from that which existed in the beginning before this cell manifested in physical form, which was, and is, awareness from the void.

When coming into manifestation from the implosion and the explosion, and then the second explosion, there came a geometric fractal light blueprint.

Depending on the nature of the vibration, each vibration has its own geometry, and in each state there is always going to be change. All is in a state of constant change. From the geometric light blueprint, we are now seeing a change in our solar system with the temperatures and Earth changes. All this comes from the light blueprint.

From the first galaxy came a ripple and fractal geometry creating the other galaxies, which are vibrating on a continuum and manifesting from the light blueprint. In time, you will see how everything ending, beginning, and in-between is set out geometrically. What's been done here has also been done in other galaxies.

We learn, evolve, and continue to grow, and this evolution has gotten to a pinnacle at this time with Earth. You have volunteered to be here and help with the next phase, the Shift, and it's up to you as to how you want to proceed and where you want to go. If you want to ascend this facet of yourself through the vibrations and colors of the Light Body, you can do it by recognizing, understanding, and reconnecting to God's mind, your mind.

You are the Elohim and the Elohim is a cell of Source. In this way, you *are* Source. You might feel like you have amnesia, sometimes, but it is only because of the vibration here—which you are now changing and lifting. You have a multidimensional mind. This is a self-mastery experience. Remember, your mind is God's mind.

January 11, 2017

Shi-Ji via Peter Maxwell Slattery

Chapter 2
The First Humans in Lyra

The first human life came into being in this galaxy from the Elohim state by manifesting in the Constellation Lyra. Originally, through the human experience, there were challenges and the gleaning of knowledge and experience, which then went to the oversoul and Source for the overall collective. But gradually there were those who fell, and this changed everything.

The stories in your ancient texts, such as those in the Judeo-Christian Bible, contain some truth, although a large percentage of it has been manipulated. The stories of those who have fallen also contain some truth. The origin of these stories is in Lyra, and it's a repeat of what has been done in other realms throughout the universe.

From the Elohim light blueprint of this reality (which manifested through thought), the Light Body cell divided and came into this vibration in Lyra. Gradually, through losing the oneness, there came manipulation, greed, and many other negative traits. Unfortunately, this has been repeated here. Then, from the fear trap created by those who did not want to return to the Elohim state—because they lost their connection to Source—came the creation of the Artificial Intelligence in this galaxy. It was already in existence in other galaxies, because the same thing was happening elsewhere, over and over again.

The Artificial Intelligence that was created in this galaxy linked up to other Artificial Intelligence devices and networks (which are multidimensional) in many other galaxies. A device was created to hold a vibration the other worlds do not experience easily—although through intention anyone can experience them.

This was done to keep those who were not connected to Source blind to the greater reality, and keep humans from connecting to Source (although you always are). It was done so those who fell could run, rule, and dominate this realm and appear to be God-like.

The Lower Light and its soldiers, the Artificial Intelligence, parasitic thought forms, and those in line with them are fed through the energy they create by domination, and through fear, lust, greed, and other lower vibrations.
Some of you became aware of "The God within" through your knowingness of right and wrong of a greater reality,

Great division was created between the factions of those who were coming from the position of self-service mode and ego, because they all wanted more power.

Eventually, Reptilians from other galaxies and the Draco Constellation came into knowledge of the humans in Lyra. At that time, other humans from other galaxies were looking in on what was happening here, once they knew of the humans in this galaxy. Once aware, they began monitoring and visiting certain Beings.

More wars broke out among the Lyran races on a bigger scale than ever before. At that time, there were many types of humans and other life forms in Lyra.

Most humans were twenty to thirty feet tall, and they were Nordic, melanin dominant. There were many other races of different colors: red, green, blue, and yellow, although those who first came into manifestation were what you would call a tanned/bronze color. Depending on their planet and various conditions, they adapted to the environment and physical changes, and differences in skin color, hair, and so on started to happen. Eventually, they spread out in Lyra.

War broke out among many factions because of division and the desire for individual sovereignty. This is the result of the Reptilians coming into the system. The Reptilians wanted to take over what the humans had created; they wanted domination over most human groups. They set up alliances and war broke out, which eventually led to the explosion of a star from a bomb. This eventually destroyed the planets in the star's system. Around this time, the manipulation and Reptilian mind was introduced to humans in this sector.

Most were wiped out. There were some who had left before the wars took place; they wanted no part of it. Some were in huge motherships already docked on the far reaches of Lyra because they had foreseen what was going to happen. These groups were in service mode.

Also, some Beings had moved long beforehand over to Vega, which is local to Lyra. Some had already come into Being from the light blueprint (through thought) by the Elohim before the Lyra Wars.

After some regrouping, those who were evolved and wanted to explore the galaxy went out and set up outposts and civilizations throughout Orion, Hyades, Sirius, Andromeda Constellation, Arcturus, Aldebaran, the Pleiades, many other places, and eventually Earth. This happened in many densities.

For the most part, most knew about their heritage and what had happened in Lyra. They never again wanted to recreate a similar situation. There was still the Lower Light in human form roaming around going rogue, and this still happens from time to time.

Eventually, there were the Orion Wars. This was twofold and based on greed. In part, it was a race war between humans against humans, and also a war against the Reptilians, the Lower Light, and the Artificial Intelligence.

Based on knocking out the Empire, which was located near the star in Orion's Belt, it eventually spread out across the Orion Constellation far and wide. The Orions created an alliance with the Sirians and other parties from other systems. After the race war ended, the focus was on the Reptilians, the Lower Light, and the Artificial Intelligence.

The wars lasted for thousands of years and no one won. There was a stalemate. The Reptilians left and the humans who were involved died off. However, many lived for one to two thousand years.

The Human Orions were coming at the issue of war from a higher level of conciseness. The issue of war died out for them, just like the many lives it took. They became protectors of justice, warriors, and spiritually advanced Beings.

Before and during the wars, The Orion Council of Light was monitoring this episode with other civilizations and warning all involved about how destabilizing war would be, both physically and spiritually. But greed took over. No one listened to the Council. By this time, defense was needed because the Reptilians, the Lower Light, and the Artificial Intelligence refused to agree. Many lives were taken.

After the Orion Wars, two more head Councils were created in Arcturus and the Andromeda Constellation to monitor and mediate between all the groups in this sector of space. This led to many local groups joining the Andromeda Galaxy Council.

Gradually, all parts of the Councils came to know what the other parts were doing, and they started working together in a peaceful, diplomatic way to help and assist each other. Those who did not participate on the same level did not receive assistance. Many were free to join if they wanted to, although they needed to be in a higher state of consciousness, so as to not upset the balance, destabilize, or impose on lesser-evolved civilizations.

After the Orion Wars in your solar system, there were civilizations on the planets Melona/Maldek, Mars, and Earth. Outposts were located on all planetary bodies and most of the moons, too. Some of the moons are crafts (UFOs) that once were natural objects. The placing of these objects around planets helped to manipulate environments so life would be comfortable on some planets. Others are used for this reason, too, but also as weapons to protect environments and secure life after the Orion and Lyra Wars.

The Reptilians, the Lower Light, and the Artificial Intelligence affected those on Melona/Maldek. A bomb was let off, which turned the planet into the asteroid belt you see today in your solar system. Mars was blown out of its orbit, and those who survived either went underground on Mars or came to Earth.

Originally, about twenty million years ago, the Lyrans had outposts and small colonies on Earth, Mars, and Melona/Maldek. Eventually, Earth became the cradle of civilization in this solar system. The Lyrans are the Anunnaki, and in truth, the Anunnaki are the Elohim.

Some Beings visited for diplomatic purposes through the Councils, when visiting Earth from Orion, Sirius, The Pleiades, Arcturus, Hyades, the Andromedas, and many other places.

Descendants of the Lyrans still had a strong hold on Earth and the solar system after arriving here around twenty million years ago. They created a huge civilization on Earth about 500,000 years ago and manipulated the first Beings here through thought. They mixed themselves with these Beings. In time, the Pleiadians did this, too.

Many civilizations grew and fell, time and time again. Then, about 380,000 thousand years ago, the Reptilians arrived on Earth. About 230,000 years ago, a group of Pleiadians came across the civilizations of their ancestors here and started monitoring what was going on.

It was known by those in the Councils that the Reptilians were manipulating the humans on Earth with assistance from the Artificial Intelligence. At one time, there was an agreement that allowed the Reptilians to be here and get along with the humans. When the manipulation was understood, a ship with a collective of Beings came here to visit and confront the situation, which had been agreed to by the Councils and the Reptilians. It was a set-up.

The Reptilians shot it down in space, and the ship changed its makeup in the outer atmosphere and became what we know as Moldavite. There were a few types created from this event because of the conditions. Some is in and around the Czech Republic and some is in Australia, which is where this craft crashed. After this event, the Reptilian group was dealt with accordingly and had to live with the guilt. The Lower Light and the Artificial Intelligence continued the manipulation later.

In the meantime, an opportunity arose for the Pleiadians to start creating civilizations on Earth. These civilizations became known as Atlantis and Lemuria. Both of them grew to be all over the world. For some time, they got along. It wasn't until later that the Atlantians lost the knowledge of their heritage, and then spiritual knowledge and balance. This allowed the Reptilians, the Lower Light, and the Artificial Intelligence to overshadow them.

Meanwhile, many civilizations that were lost in the Pleiades from the wars, or in exploring space, came across each other and created multiple civilizations near multiple stars in the Pleiades. There is a collective of civilizations in this area with many different types of races. They live in peace and assist others in the universe through thought, and through visiting when appropriate. Thus, there is an effort to make sure what happened in Orion and Lyra never happens again.

Eventually, the behavior of the Atlantians became very disturbing. They started experimenting on their own people and mixing animals and humans together, which went against Universal law. They wanted control over the Earth, the solar system, and beyond. Working in line with the Reptilians, the Lower Light, and the Artificial Intelligence, they decided to take the path of *service to self*. The Lemurians took the opposite path: *service to others*.

When Atlantis lost its way, some of the Lemurians were on guard, watching and keeping an open heart. However the friendship between Atlantis and Lemuria died and, with no warning, the Atlantians destroyed the main Lemurian capital. This time war broke out. The Lemurians had always kept their spiritual connection, stayed in service mode, were very spiritually advanced, and had some advanced technology, but this hit them hard.

The Atlantians continued on their path of destruction, as they dissolved and wiped out the homes, towns, and cities of the Lemurians. The Lemurians had a craft in space, which they used for the purpose of monitoring, doing research, and space defense. In defense against the Atlantians, they beamed the tracker onto a piece of asteroid from the asteroid belt, and then slammed it right into the hub of the Atlantian civilization. This ended the war instantly.

Before this and during their downfall, the Atlantians had destroyed some of their own popular locations because of crazy experiments done by their scientists. These experiments did not turn out to be productive for the overall collective.

After the fall of Lemuria and Atlantis, the Earth was uninhabitable. Even those who had become Inner Earth Beings, going back twenty million years, had a hard time staying here, but they took in some of the Lemurians. Some of the Atlantians continued on in a base in Antarctica. Some went off-world to Mars and other places. The Bigfoot races worldwide were devastated, as were the nature realms, spirits, and Gaia.

Eventually, some of the Atlantians and other warring races came back to Earth to manipulate. This is where your Mahabharata and some of the stories in the Bible, the Quran, and your other texts came from. (These texts were later manipulated.) The wars in your ancient texts, with all your so-called gods and demi-gods, are a continuation of the ancient wars.

Eventually, the Reptilians, the Lower Light, and the Atlantians came back strong. They came back to manipulate through psychic attacks on the populace with great precision and timing, but this time it was through the Nazi agenda.

Although it might seem like the Nazis are gone, Earth is still engaged in this battle. It appears that through "Project Paper Clip," the Nazi scientists were either absorbed by the U.S.A. or taken by the Russians, put on trial, or killed. Although some of this did happen, most of it was a smokescreen. The Nazis continued with their agenda in Antarctica at the Atlantian base. Some of the heads of America, Britain, and others know this behind the scenes. With their space fleets, they now go out into space to rebuild and contribute to the Lower Light and Artificial Intelligence.

Now we are up to today, and the flipside is that because we are all one consciousness, we have created this experience, this self-mastery experience. Through thought, we created all this as a collective.

Similar events have occurred in other galaxies, and now those in service are creating a conscious grid here on Earth—and also universally for the ascension of those who are ready for the next level of consciousness.

Love, gratitude, and empathy are needed in these times, and also maintaining a non-reactionary state of mind. This is the greatest experience and operation of all.

You are the "anti-virus" to the manipulative "virus" that will lead to the next stage of your growth and evolution, and also the overall collective's growth and evolution in this dimension, universe, and beyond.

January 12, 2017
Shi-Ji via Peter Maxwell Slattery

Chapter 3
Manifesting Your Tomorrow

Now is the time to create your reality. The change you seek is only a thought away. Changing your tomorrow starts with the mind, your thoughts. Through observing your thoughts and your awareness, you can manifest the tomorrow you desire and feel in your heart. The human experience is multidimensional, and when you are in non-linear mind you can change the past, present, and future. Even your epigenetics can change.

Through intention and connecting to the God within, working on yourself, your practices, and intention, you can change your epigenetics, your ancestors' epigenetics, and your offspring's epigenetics, because you are multidimensional and everything is in symbiotic relationship.

The traits you already have, manifest, create, and work on are also in the epigenetics of your ancestors and offspring. You can affect the past, present, and future when you recognize and understand this. Just as your ancestors' epigenetics affect you today, you can affect theirs and your future offspring's reality.

For manifestation to come into being, you must first be able to come from a place of love and no judgment. You must also forgive yourself and others, and have empathy and compassion for all, including yourself.

Before you can be of use to others, you need to look after yourself in mind, body, and spirit. You need to release the past and learn the lessons from it. Your past contains all the teachings you have and will experience.

See the good and beautiful in all creation and have brotherly, sisterly, and self-love. For this, forgiveness is the key. Intention is another. Love is another. Service is another. And open-mindedness is another.

Feel your human emotions. Don't block them out, because they are there for the self-mastery experience. You will be tested, which is also part of the human experience.

The human experience is more intense and heightened than any other because of what seem like limitations. All of this is an illusion. The Illusion of fear is just an emotion. After recognizing how this reality works, your experiences and what you attract will depend on your vibration. Love is the only true vibration, and when resonating with truth, love is necessary to connect with Source and your God self, because Source resonates as one with the love frequency.

Yes...the Reptilian brain/mind has infiltrated the human experience. This was done to add to the self-mastery experience, although it has been more of a blessing than a burden. It's a blessing in disguise, because once you master how it works, it will contribute to the strength of your mind, thoughts, and reactions. You can learn how to react from your heart by observing and recognizing your thoughts.

Most humans react automatically to their thoughts, instead of recognizing them and the intention and action behind them. When you are in reactionary mind and not paying attention to your thoughts, events can manifest that you would rather do without.

You can see examples in humanity's past from wars and abuse in whatever form. This is what manifests from thought when we are in reactionary mind, when we do not observe our thoughts first and then react from the heart. When you observe your thoughts, you will have a choice in how you react.

Parasitic thought forms, Reptilians with ill intent, the Lower Light, and others aligned with self-service have an advantage over those who are not aware of their thoughts, where their thoughts come from, and their actions. This is how these Beings can affect and manipulate their prey. They create energy to feed the Artificial Intelligence and themselves, in order to keep the love frequencies at a maximum distance. In this way, they can continue to exist and rule in this vibration. It's more of a "thought war" than anything else, and it affects everyone's sovereignty, happiness, health, and freedom.

You have assistance at this time from other facets of yourself, your Guides, and the Beings you work with on multiple levels. Light cities exist outside your frequency on Earth, and they are filled with multiple Beings who are assisting with the conscious grid. The Brotherhood of Light, the many types of Councils, and the many Guardians—and also the Ancient Spirits in all portal areas—are here to help and assist humanity.

Many Beings from many other places and universes are helping to monitor and protect the Earth, while holding and contributing to the energy grid here. These helpers include: the Pleiadians, Orions, Sirians, Arcturians, Andromedans, a whole host of Beings from the Star Nations in this galaxy and beyond, and also the Ascended Beings, who are in their ships and Light Bodies docked around the Earth, your solar system, and beyond. These Ascended Beings contribute and help hold space for humanity, and for all those who have come here to assist.

The vibration and geometry are changing the electromagnetic energy in your part of space, solar system, and galaxy. The whole vibration of your plane is changing. You can see for yourself that the Earth's magnetic field is weakening. This weakening of the electromagnetic field is the result of a vibrational change. In time, you will come into a more null zone of electromagnetic energy. This is part of the shift. Everything is changing and you can access anything you need to know by working on yourself. In time your part in all of this will become clear.

The pineal gland is crystalline in nature. It is also multidimensional and, as such, it's a transmitter and receiver. Everything works on a light waveform that is manifested from the Elohim geometric light blueprint.

You are alive in an electric universe! It is made up of energy. The electromagnetic component is changing, and the blueprint and geometry of it is changing, too. It's going to vibrate like never before, and soon another channel (or vibration)` will come from it. Then it will divide like a cell and create another density, like a mother giving birth. For this to happen, the timelines had to come together, and now we are going into another stage of evolution. Everything has electron and photon components and is holographic in nature.

For some time now, multidimensional artifacts like the obelisks and pyramids have been seen in your towns, cities, and countries. They also exist on other planets, moons, suns, the stars in this galaxy, and beyond. Some of them were created to assist humanity, such as the crystalline, multidimensional pyramids created by the Elohim. Most of you do not know about them because of the numbing of most of the human senses, multidimensional mind, and the pineal gland. They hold a vibration so they can come through easily and be noticed by those who are ready. The ancient structures and the layout of many ancient cities are also artifacts, and even modern cities on earth and beyond could be considered artifacts.

We are speaking of energy circuits and transmitters. When looked at from above, you will see they look like circuit boards. The energy from these devices feeds energy to the Lower Light Network and the Artificial Intelligence, which are multidimensional.

When you drive on your roads and walk the paths across the world, they link up to everything and the energy goes into the obelisks you see around your populace in plain sight. The tops of towers, skyscrapers, churches, and the food courts in your malls and shopping centers are all doing the same thing: taking human emotional energy and sending it into the atmosphere to feed the Artificial Intelligence grid.

The energies in your environment serve, recycle, and continue to feed this network. From the energy of wanting possessions to expressions of ego, these are the things this system thrives on—and places like your malls and shopping centers teach, promote, and thrive on this energy, too. In effect, this actually attracts the food source to feed the grid through the brainwashing of society. You are here to break this grid and help it implode on itself.

As these things are coming to light, over many years much has been amped up from both sides of the war. Implants and Nano technology are being used by the negative forces that control the populace, and also Black Ops, Super Soldiers, the Secret Space Program, and those working with the Reptilians and other self-serving races. In other words, Artificial Intelligence and the Lower Light have many resources.

On a multilayered level, implants of an energetic and physical nature have been placed, in some cases, in order to transfer negative emotional energy from humans (fear and hate, for example) to the lower vibrations and feed their grid.

There are undercover soldiers who slow down operations inside programs, divert discussions, and watch out for those who are a threat to the Lower Light's established order. These are your comrades in arms. They are also helping the overall collective, because the Lower Light should not be hated and looked down upon, but be loved, because this shift is ultimately for them, too.

By the Lower Light doing what it does, in time you will understand that this is what makes us come at obstacles from a higher level of consciousness in dealing with certain situations. Once we recognize this, we will be open and achieve a higher level of understanding. As a cell of a greater intelligence, we will grow, thrive, and become far more evolved as we move on to greater experiences and states of consciousness.

Distorted, inverted awareness is the polar opposite of your human vibration. Your point of attention is all that matters and where real change manifests.

It's about reconnecting and coming from the heart. From the heart, you can create a new vibrational geometric blueprint that will get absorbed into the blueprint that is already here. In effect, this creates another new vibrational blueprint that holds all possibilities. Doing this with love is the key.

Humans are a source of energy for the Lower Light Network. The original humans and many others in your past have known this. The Lower Light has used multidimensional technology to dumb down humans, because humans are capable of being more spiritual advanced than they are. If humans were aware of just a spark of their true nature, they would be enlightened instantly.

The brain, heart, and gut emotions must be recognized, because these are the physical components of multidimensional emotions, and they are transmitters of change. To get to the point, it all has to do with you and your thoughts and intentions. These messages are only helping you to remember what you already know. You are Gods and you are multidimensional! You are the hands and feet of God and cells of the infinite.

Frustration, being upset, worrying, fear, and control—these are the traits you must learn to simply observe. Don't contribute to that which you are trying to change. Be the observer and the author of your reality, and make a positive contribution.

Do not assume or think you know everything. Be open-minded at all times to all possibilities so you can be effective here. Do clearings; observe your thoughts and what comes through. Are your thoughts coming from your Higher Self, your God-self, or other facets of yourself? Are you in service mode or something else? Are you productive, or not? Do your thoughts produce fruit that will grow and flourish, or do they produce sick, ill-colored fruit from the geometric light blueprint?

These are the telltale signs that will show you whether what you are connecting with is in line with your highest good.

Nothing is more evolved, helpful, or more of service than your own God self, because this is the all-knowing, nonjudgmental, ultimate guide and teacher—although it is also still learning and evolving in the vibration of love.

Focusing on your awareness will help you connect with your own God self. Observing your thoughts, sounds, and smells (everything you can sense) is a connecting point to the mind of God. Everything has to do with awareness.

Pay attention to how you observe life around you. Are you focused and aware? If you get to a place in which you realize you are looking into this reality, then backtrack, knowing you are going to God's mind (which is your mind). From there you can manifest your tomorrow.

January 13, 2017

Shi-Ji via Peter Maxwell Slattery

The Book of Shi-Ji 2

Chapter 4
Humanity's Future

It's up to you to decide whether you will be your own master and in charge of the reality you create. It's your choice.

Change starts within you, and from there it projects outside of you. The more you work on yourself, the more your positive change will wear off on others and they will do the same. From this point, the results will move to collective consciousness. Critical mass is the key! Those of you who are here to help are portals for new energies and vibrations. You are the links to help humanity help itself.

There are many ways the coming changes will manifest, and it will be different for many humans. Some will stay; some will go into another vibrational reality here. Some will go elsewhere completely, and some will ascend. It's very layered. Each will be able to go where they want to go for this facet of soul development.

Some will see planets, artificial objects, and moons in your solar system, which will be nonexistent for others—their environments will be different. Some of you will see Beings with many different characteristics, while others will not. Some of you might experience heightened abilities and be able to communicate with wildlife, plants, and trees, and have a dialogue with them in ways like never before. You might even connect and communicate with the Earth, the universe, and your own God self. These changes will come in many ways and will take many forms.

There will be a slow leak of disclosure for mainstream society. This has already begun, because many are looking outside of themselves for authority and disclosure. A slow leak is coming about our advances in space, the space stations, Mars, achievements in relation to Mars, and other exciting events.

More news on possible life and radio signals from elsewhere, other Earth-like planets, and past UFO events by your governments worldwide—these things being thrown out to the masses through mainstream news and they are slowly opening people up to the inevitable, the truth. What's going on is too deep for most people to fathom completely at this time.

Those who are aware of what's going on will guide their fellow brothers and sisters. Communication with otherworldly Beings will not be what most humans believe it to be, but you will assist with this reality, too. Overnight, the realization of the change will shock some. At the individual level, working on your conscious awareness is the key to increasing your development.

The thoughts and vibrations of most people do not resonate with the Beings in less dense planes, so it's hard for some Beings to be around humans here. In the same way, it is uncomfortable for some Earth Humans to be open to other Beings, because humans keep secrets and their thoughts are hidden. Much will change!

You can communicate at any time with your Guides, Higher Self, friends from other planes, extraterrestrials, Inner Earth, and multidimensional Beings. Look at it like this: Do you want to communicate with what is near and just above your level of consciousness, or do you want to evolve and connect with those who are evolved, in service mode, and can help you reconnect to your own God self? Remember to use discernment at all times.

Technologies will change in the coming days. The ripping up of the energy grid will occur because it will be wireless and free. This means we will go to zero point energy, which has no emissions and comes from the fabric of space, so it won't affect us negatively like microwaves and 5G. Food, water, shelter, clothing, and everything else you need will be provided.

Jobs in all areas to help the collective evolve will be provided, and the jobs will be exciting for those doing them, because people will be doing what they love. Transport, entertainment, love, friendships, family life, health—all this and more will be affected.

Robots, droids, and drones will be doing most of the work. They will be designed and created by humans, so humans can learn and go out into space and other realms, while learning new ways to do things and supporting the new lifestyle. Humans will be taught the skills they need to accomplish whatever they desire and are good at doing.

There will be next level symbiotic technologies that will be *living* technology. There will also be a balance of spiritual advancement and technological advancement because of the level of consciousness of the Earth Humans. At the moment, however, this is not how it is. Everything is leading to a transhumanism agenda for those on this vibration. There is going to be a "snap," and it is not far off, because the Lower Light and its allies are not able to evolve any further. They are at their maximum capacity for knowledge and advancement because of their limited level of consciousness.

With great knowledge comes discernment, and humanity must first do all this itself. There are Guides and a multidimensional mind assisting you, so take advantage of both.

From a higher level of consciousness, rape, murder, injustice, greed, and the like do not exist, because these negative things cannot exist when there is a high level of consciousness. They do not occur because there is mastery of the mind and a change in the body computer and software. Humans are amazing Beings, capable of a new, higher level of consciousness. But you are no more special than any other Beings, even though what you are capable of is beyond your wildest dreams.

This is why some of the hybrid kids are Light Beings, and why there are even hybrid Elohim Beings. They are the result of what humans can do. Many races are connecting with the light blueprint of your bodies and mixing it with theirs to take back to their realms. They add this to their Light Bodies so they can glean some of the amazing abilities and traits that humans have. These Beings have great mastery of mind and intention, so this human contribution to their Light Bodies and to the overall collective is incredible, because the Beings doing this are in service mode.

Transhumanism is a tool for the Artificial Intelligence to feed the Lower Light Network grid.

The Transhumanism agenda was created to stop you on many levels from connecting to who you are, which contributes to the Lower Light and their existence.

Cell phone towers, Morgellons disease, chemtrails, nano bots, wi-fi, Haarp, fluoride, smart dust, computer chips, smart glasses, psyops, the drug industry, GMOs, and the like are all tools that do what they were created for—stop you from connecting with your own God self, all possibilities, and the frequency of love and truth.

Some say the goal of transhumanism is to allow you exist forever, but the truth is you will exist forever in many forms and ways, more than you can even imagine.

In effect, the Artificial Intelligence is part of this cell, which is a cell of a greater intelligence. It exists because we allow it. It serves its purpose because of the huge positive affect it has in making you think in an expansive way, which leads to a higher level of consciousness. In other words, you are raising your consciousness in an attempt to defeat the Artificial Intelligence.

Even though some of those who serve this system appear to be Gods, they are not. Just look at how they are external and look outside of themselves. Child abuse, trauma, sacrifices and rituals, the knowledge of astronomy and astrology, letters, and symbols—all of this carries energy. They know how to manipulate all this and use it for their benefit. This, in turn, contributes to the Lower Light and their allies, and feeds their network.

Astronomy, planetary knowledge, and astrology can also be used for good. This means not going outside of yourself, but rather simply using this knowledge as a tool to help amplify that which you desire. As long as you are in service mode and have a positive agenda with regard to what you are doing, using this knowledge will be beneficial because it means you are going with the flow and using the current of abundance whenever the opportunity arises.

This is why those who are negative use it to assist them, because the energies help them manifest their goals and feed their grid. Over time, this has a negative effect, because they rely on it and not their own God self.

What happens to humanity is up to each individual and the collective. There are many possibilities: the

New Earth, the New Realm, a post-disclosure world, or the same world. It depends on your intention, point of focus, and awareness because you view reality through your own lens in deciding what to chose or manifest.

You are here to bring the state of Source to this realm, and all realms, before this cell of a greater intelligence regenerates. How you eat, how you sleep, how you function, and more, will be different in the coming times. Connecting to your thoughts, observing them, discernment with regard to them, and coming from a place of love are the keys for your evolution.

Your insecurities are tools to look at yourself and recognize the gifts you have for others and yourself. Your good deeds do not go unnoticed. You build your riches in the heavenly planes, not here, although it can help in this plane because what goes around comes around on an energetic level.

Treat your body as your temple, because it is a temple in this realm. With your point of focus here, remember your mind is multidimensional. Lookout for yourself, because just as humanity has to achieve a higher level of consciousness, so do humans on an individual level.

This is first a self-mastery experience, which then leads to a collective mastery experience. With both, you have to become the observer and see things for what they are, which is Source interacting with itself.

Monks might be enlightened in their temples behind closed doors—where they are without temptations from the outside world—but can they carry these traits out into the real world without a controlled environment? If so, this defines them as Masters. You must be able to function in both the world and beyond. Be an observer and guide others in helping themselves. Keep this as your primary intention.

These are true tests: being in service and observing your mind. Strive to recognize and understand this so you can achieve whatever you choose. Are you ready to reach your goals? Are you happy with your present life?

There is no right or wrong answer, and it's up to you to decide where you want your future to take you, and what you would like to see, explore, and experience. Humanity is capable of so much and it has all the tools and skills it needs to evolve. You are the master of your destiny, and humanity is the master of its own destiny, as a collective.

Non-linear mind is of key importance here, and so are persistence, being nonjudgmental, open-mindedness, love, and nonattachment. You are your own best teacher, and your experiences really have everything to do with only you—and later the overall collective, because ultimately everything leads to the collective. Poor, rich, black, white, tall, or small—none of it matters because all are facets of your experiences—and all is Source. So...do your best. Set your intentions on whatever is the most important to you, and your evolution will also benefit the evolution of humanity.

Other people might abuse you, use you, and take advantage of you. These are two of your lessons: (1) learn to say no, and (2) trust your thoughts and intuition. There are those who will cross the line and try to break your free will, so use your judgment in each case. And then take your knowledge to humanity as a whole.

Are you doing something to change your actions, attitude, and intentions, or do you just complain? Are you contributing to the collective good by playing your part and going with the flow? The future is in your hands. You are your own Master.

January 14, 2017
Shi-Ji via Peter Maxwell Slattery

Chapter 5
Assistance and Protection

Humanity is experiencing the next level of vibrational change with a Master vibration, which all other vibrations resonate within. The changing phase and place between frequencies is on the same inter-plane.

The Christ vibration is the connection to Source, and it's an encompassing plane with many mansions. One of the few code and key sounds of Source is "Om." This is one of the few ways to connect with Source's vibration, which flows with love and bliss. Like everything else, it is constructed by light.

The Throne Beings who work in sync with the Elohim, the Angelics, the Councils, and the Guardians are situated in the vibration of Source that sits on the outskirts of the geometric vibrations. They are structured by light.

When possessing a higher level of consciousness, the keys to the ascension worlds allow the facet of you that has ascended to create its own universe if it chooses to do so. At this stage, light codes and sounds shine the flame of light from Source and pave the way for your oversoul to divide off. These light codes and sounds are multidimensional and are only available to those who are ready to access and handle what comes with them. They are Universal.

Once you are at a certain level of consciousness, you will become one with the Source vibration on a noticeable level. At this stage, your God self will create your own universe, with its planes, realms, vibrations, and inter-planes, and you will divide off from the geometric light blueprint, like a cell divides, and create your own universe.

Even though everything is part of a collective and comes from one construct, each has its own uniqueness. The feminine, the masculine, the Earth, and planetary bodies, moons, stars, and galaxies all play their part.

Everything in the universe is made of light that vibrates at different frequencies. This light creates awareness, highlighting the symbiotic, illusionary, holographic nature and reality of the universe. We have access to everything that exists, and the restraints we have that prevent us from opening depend on what we allow to manifest from the blueprint state.

Assistance is only a thought away. Remember...part of the Earth human experience is the self-mastery journey to rediscovering oneself. Everything you create is from the blueprint level.

Through embodying love and expressing your love, care, empathy, and being in service mode, you are like children going with the flow. Your love creates a link, a vibration that resonates within you, providing an opportunity (through thought) for your Guides and other facets to come through. This is all up to you. You must do the work, and humanity as a collective has to do its work, until the many manifestations created from disclosure, ascension, the New Earth, and higher states of consciousness come into being.

Throne Beings of Light, other Beings constructed of light, your ancestors in this vibration, those who are neutral, and mediators—all can communicate with you, and assist you in helping yourself. The tricksters, the Artificial Intelligence and the Lower Light Network, will use those who have not done the work to connect with the higher vibrations to assist in their negative agendas.

From your point of awareness in the human body, you can connect to your Higher Self, your Guides, fellow Beings, facets, extra and ultra-dimensional Beings, and the like. They are here to assist you, although discernment must be used at all times. All that is required is for you to make the effort to connect with your Higher Self. The helpers communicate through numbers, synchronicities, and your thoughts, and they can come through whenever needed, if you are open to them.

Those who want to meet other facets of themselves through intention can slowly reconnect and bring through traits from the other realms and other facets, which will contribute to the awakening and healing process. The choice is up to you. No judgment or pressure comes with this. You know what you should do. You know right from wrong without being told.

The Golden Lion Beings from Sirius and the light blueprint geometry connecting them to their brothers and sisters in Orion and Lyra are here to assist and protect you. They are from the realms constructed of light. The Golden Lion Beings are back here to protect and assist you, and also Michael.

They were gone for some time, but they are slowly reconnecting into this plane at the thought transfer level. They are manifesting and showing themselves to those they work with and the advisers of that which they protect and serve. They are back because many of you are here in service mode. Their job is to serve as bodyguards for those who know and recognize the God within, and who are in service mode.

Aligning and balancing your chakras, feeding and realigning the light body, resting it, cleansing it, and cleaning it—you must do these things for your

Merkabah to bring through direct, fresh, new communication on a recognizable level, from their blueprint to yours, because they overlap.

Everything you experience, or not, is for a reason. Your many lives in the other planes, the many other facets of self that you might be experiencing or having interactions with are purposeful. Some of you are the Angelic Beings you speak of, because they can split up and put a facet of themselves into a human body here and/or elsewhere. They can also be in multiple places at the same time. All Beings can do this when reconnecting and rising to a higher level of consciousness.

The pearls in the sky from the ancient text of Buddha, ancient art depicting Jesus and other Beings in white, rainbows, blue orbs, and even

Beings coming from the Elohim vibration—all this tells of or depicts true events.

Ascension, your mysteries, and all of multidimensional existence have been known since your ancient times and even further.

Everything is an offshoot from another; it's fractal, although everything is smaller than the eye of a needle, because it is happening in Source's Eye, God's Eye. All is a form of manifestation in the photon. There is much for you to do and experience from the Elohim—the gatekeeper and the key to connecting to other universes and to Source.

At this time, other Beings from other universes have come through the eye of their cell of Source to ours because everything is in symbiotic relationship. They have been allowed to do this because of their intention to assist here in a productive manner. Some have split off a facet of self and focused that point of their attention and awareness into a human body to help hold energy and contribute to the evolution of Earth.

This is what Gods do, and you can, too. So lose yourself to find yourself, while being of service and assistance to others. In a sense, you have accepted the assignment to help on the multidimensional level.

You create from your thoughts. From the light of your consciousness comes whatever you decide to manifest through thought. If you understand this, you can remove, delete, and dissolve anything. This is how the Saints, Sages and Masters of old (who still exist) create and manifest from thought.

Sometimes you might have unpleasant experiences. This is part of what you signed up for, or they might be situations and events created by your oversoul to steer you towards something you agreed to before coming into this plane.

As the layers peel away, so will what you once thought you knew or understood. This is where being open-minded, nonjudgmental, and using your discernment will help you to help yourself and, in turn, help others to experience, know, and reconnect to all possibility.

You are not your body. You are not your thoughts. You are not what others think of you. You are all that is, has, and ever will be, having an experience through a point of awareness, focused through a lens here, and having this experience in what those coming from linear mind call "time."

Everything happens for a reason, not by coincidence. Everything has already happened and is happening at the same time. Everything is accessible by thought, because all is flowing through the electromagnetic current of Source.

Everything has an electromagnetic component (within the electron), which is symbiotic to all that is overseen by Metatron, the Master and regulator of the electron from the geometric light blueprint vibration.

Many of your Guides and others who assist you are already with you. Some even walk among you. They are your friends, family, and colleagues, those you surround yourself with. Yes...some come and some go. How you learn, what tools you gleaned, the love you have for others—these are the things that are stored in the book of knowledge with all that is. They are never forgotten. They contribute to the understanding of the overall collective.

You are never alone in your mind, in your thoughts, or in your surroundings. Everything is noticed. Always watch your thoughts, ideas, and signs, because this is how we let you know we are with you. Let what comes through flow when setting the intent to connect with us. Even if what comes through does not make sense, it will, in time. Have balance in all you do and be open to receive in all areas. If not, you will create a block to that which you seek.

See your weaknesses as strengths, and the blessings and burdens as one and the same, because both will help you on your journey. Accept the negative, and recognize everything that is right. Love, don't fight. This you already know.

When things go sour or stale, make changes, because this opens the way for new energies and the next level to come through. Recognize the old and welcome the new. Appreciate and have gratitude for both. Everything is part of your journey. Things happen when the energies align—you will understand this through the synchronicities in your journeys.

Always clear your energies and thoughts regularly. Recognize when you need help. Even when you are your own master, you sometimes need to recognize that you must be a follower, too, in order to learn from others. Surround yourself with that which is in line with your intentions, service, growth, fun, and love.

Know that your Higher Self and all who work with you are sending the vibration of love to you through the geometric light blueprint. They are telling you that they are proud of you and that you are loved and never alone. They are cheering you on. They—the beautiful many—are always there and nothing goes unnoticed.

You are your own judge. Anything you have done and don't like is only for you, and you alone. What you get from your experiences is up to you. Know that everything you experience is also for the overall collective. Everyone makes mistakes. This is part of the human self-mastery learning experience.

Go to your heart, the vibration of love. This will allow you to recognize everything that serves you, just as you serve others, whether you recognize it or not. Everyone has what you call a Guardian Angel. This is actually another facet of you. Open your heart and mind, and set the intention to know your Guardian Angel.

We are always with you. Just take notice of the first thing that comes to mind when setting your intention to connect. We are in your thoughts, just as you are in ours. God's mind and your mind are one and the same.

January 15, 2017

Shi-Ji via Peter Maxwell Slattery

The Book of Shi-Ji 2

Chapter 6

Ascension, Energy Waves, and Opportunities

There have been opportunities for some time to help you adapt and bring into focus that which no longer serves you. These new opportunities have come in the form of energy, or ascension, waves.

From the higher planes and dimensions, suns and stars (which are also transmitters), these energies are just outside of the frequency here. Most of you cannot see them at this time, but they affect you physically and dimensionally in your mind, and also electromagnetically.

For some, so much is brought up when experiencing these energies. It's like what happens when there is a full moon. Everything is amplified, which also happens with planetary and star alignments.

From the moving and changing flux of geometric energies, the unseen affects all humans. The solar flares, star explosions, and solar flashes have effects on multiple levels, too. Everything is noticed, at all times, and a record of how people act and help (or not help) each other is kept in the Book of the Eternal. Understand that these experiences are self-mastery tests.

Take notice of how you purge that which no longer serves you, how you open up to new experiences, and how you observe and react your environments locally, or not.

Observe your mind. Are issues being brought up from long ago that still play in your mind? Are new goals, desires, and needs coming forth to be noticed and realized? Are you emotionally and physically drained? All these are symptoms and signs of how you are physically and emotionally adjusting and working with the new energies. How you react and take advantage of these opportunities (or not) is up to you.

You can either ride the energy waves like a surfer and use them in a productive manner, or swim against them and hold onto that which no longer serves you—stunting your evolvement process and journey—and also attract and reaffirm old patterns and programs.

Take notice of your dreams, because some of you will process your dreams and let go of that which no longer serves you. Others will foresee coming events in their dreams. Take notice of your thoughts and feelings of anger, sadness, and rage, and also happiness. Go through your emotions and process them. Recognize them, work with them, and let go of the behaviors and attitudes behind the emotions that no longer serve you. Then take the happy emotions and ride them.

Ride the bliss, because this vibration will attract new enlightenment and energies. These energy waves are opportunities to move forward and forgive. They are a blessing from Source to you.

Constant changes are happening on every level, including Earth changes and changes in the planets, moons, and stars. Your whole solar system, galaxy, and other galaxies, close, far, and beyond are being affected.

The changes are manifesting from the geometric light blueprint, which is fractal. The energies in the blueprint are constantly in motion, making change a constant. Other civilizations at your level of advancement (or at a less or more advanced stage) are going through a similar transformation. Even those throughout the other realms are experiencing similar changes. The shift is for the benefit of all.

The love frequency brings everything together because it is connected to everything. Staying in your heart center will affect everything and everyone in your environment, wherever you point your attention and awareness, and no matter what distance, because all is connected.

All of the suns and stars are connected. The portals and Beings who live on, near, and in them are connected. Regulators monitor the frequencies and activity. Throne Beings, Guardians, and many different races are watching and helping these shifts in energy. They are also helping you to help yourself.

The Artificial Intelligence was designed to block the ascension waves from your conscious mind and keep you in the dark about your true nature and your evolution process.

The media on your planet is also trying to block you, including the hypnotizing machine called the television and fake news, which doesn't cover both sides of an event or story, or use facts and discernment. Basically, you are given false stories regarding most events in order to set the agenda. And when you react to these stories, you are (in essence) giving the powers that be permission to do whatever they desire.

Everything is becoming undone because of a huge change in consciousness, including changes in the pharmaceutical industry, health food industry, entertainment, and politically.

You, who are reading this, are working and holding a vibrational frequency connected to Source. You are holding space and are part of the energy grid here at this time. The changes are evident. Unfortunately, some continue to focus on control over the human race, but the average person is slowly waking up.

People are tired of political corruption, scandals, reality TV, and the lies. They are slowly but surely becoming weary of the same misinformation and they want to know what is missing. They are realizing the sickness in their societies and they are starting to demand more self-time, and time with family, friends, and nature.

Soon the political systems and the royal families (who want to hold on to control and contribute to the Lower Light Network) will fall. This is already occurring.

Some Starseeds have incarnated into the bloodline families that hold power. They are holding positions to help assist, and when the time comes they will close down and help the people help themselves, because now is the time for each individual to govern him or herself. There will be representatives for the people and ambassadors for all areas of life. The people have agreed to this.

Corruption will be a thing of the past because thoughts will be transparent. Debating with respect and everyone's interests at heart will be the stage to sort out and network about how to move forward, solve issues, and grow as a collective, while respecting differences in cultures and belief systems.

Alliances and friendships will be abundant and everyone will keep the interests of everyone else at heart, because those you will be interacting with will be like-minded in terms of holding the intentions of service, education, love, and respect. The hearts and minds of the people will be as one. And, in time, humanity will assist and help less advanced civilizations throughout the galaxy and afar.

Through your heart and by your service to others and unity consciousness, some of you will surpass your own expectations. You will go to the Light Body or Rainbow Light Body and ascend this facet of self, surpassing the next level of consciousness. Then you will be full-blown multidimensional.

Some will even turn this facet of themselves into another oversoul, with more lives incarnating into other places and walking among other civilizations, while continuing to serve. Some might even become another oversoul, a cell of Source, and divide off and create their own universe.

During these times, you need to be strong for yourself and for those around you, who might not be as capable as you are in dealing with the evolution of your planet. You are a guide to those around you in physical form, helping them to help themselves. In one way or another, many are going to need your advice and guidance, in order to connect to the God within.

The lives of many are going to be turned upside down, inside out, and ripped to pieces. Those who don't recognize they are having or had experiences will be in a state of disbelief. This is all going to change with the events that are yet to come, have happened, and are happening.

People will need comfort and a listening ear. They will also need to be slowly educated in doing their own research and following their own journey. This is what they need until they connect with their mind, God's mind.

Moving away from the lies, tyranny, and dictatorships at the multidimensional level, humans will begin to understand how things have been and why. They will begin to excel exponentially, once they are ready to let go and go with the flow—beyond the specs of sand on your Earth, the civilizations and races out in the universe, in the other realms, and far beyond even those.

Everyone has gone through and is having revelations, trials, and tribulations. Unity consciousness does not divide. The collective will reconnect in such a way that some will not realize the human mind. Until the shift happens, humans will be at the forefront of it all, because they are a type of Super Human Being throughout the universe. They have been created in many different ways from experiments, intentions, and ideas over countless trillions of years. Yes...the Earth Human at this time is a Super Human Being.

Your prophets have spoken of the many events to come and pass. From Revelations to Armageddon, there is a war going on and many soldiers in many ways (imaginable and unimaginable) are assisting at this time.

The only way the war is going to end is through many of you reaching a higher level of consciousness. Love is the key! It is an energetic war, a war of thought, awareness, consciousness, light, vibration, and intention of individuals and the overall collective. Removing everything that stops you from connecting to the God within is required. Love, connecting to the light, and riding the bliss will assist you in beginning and following the ascension journey.

So…be open and invite those you are connected to (and your own God self) to assist you when necessary. Block out and send those Beings and entities who are not in line with you back to their highest self to be healed and release that which no longer serves them, so they can continue their own evolution.

Love is the key, and when given without conditions you can flourish and grow and spread like a tree that produces flowers, fruit, and seeds. Forgiveness, recognizing the God within, and seeing God in all creation is the way. Having your own revelation and realization in omnipresence, and seeing the creator in all creation are necessary to go to the next level.

There is no right or wrong way to proceed with your journey and development. The Lower Light is only another facet of Source, and also another facet of you.

These other facets are on their own journeys, just like you, and going their own way about it. They will eventually end up in the same place as you, once they learn to follow their bliss and reconnect and recognize the vibration of love, the vibration of truth, and step back into their sovereignty.

Each to his or her own, you are never alone. All you have to do is ask for assistance with the ascension process and it will begin.

January 16, 2017

Shi-Ji via Peter Maxwell Slattery

Chapter 7
From the Light Blueprint

Light, sound, and matter are different manifestations of consciousness and awareness. Once this is recognized, much can be understood about reality. Light, sound, and matter have a mutual symbiotic relationship. When choosing what to experience or manifest, follow the light blueprint by setting your intent. Then the experience you desire will come into play. Everything is constructed from the light blueprint.

From the light blueprint you can heal, gain knowledge, change, and manifest the reality you choose to experience. Much can be done in every way for every facet. On the opposite side, the Lower Light can also manifest from the light blueprint, although what they can do is limited because of their level of consciousness.

For example, they can put attachments on your light body (your aura). They can send parasitic thought forms that put unproductive thoughts that are not yours in your mind. You might even think these thoughts are yours, if you are not aware of the Lower Light's ability to do this.

Spells and hooks from the astral plane can be directed towards you and affect you emotionally, mentally, and physically. The self-serving Lower Light can project attachments from the light blueprint to your light body, false belief programs, and fake contracts and agreements.

Everything from a sore back, poor eyesight, headaches, sleepiness, fatigue, bursts of anger, to a range of many other things can be a manifestation from the astral plane by an attachment, Being, or implant, whether energetic or not. They can manifest many illnesses, physically and psychologically.

In order to heal, learn to avoid and block these negative projections. Focus constantly on doing clearings and connecting with your Higher self. Dissolve any entities, hooks, contracts, and agreements, known or unknown. Clear all that is not in line with you and your highest purpose on a regular basis.

Connect with your Higher Self, other facets of yourself, the beautiful many, the Beings you work with, your Guides, friends, and family in the other planes and ask for assistance when you need help.

Sometimes, the Beings you work with will take you away physically for days, weeks, or months, and then put you back at the exact second they took you, so you don't lose time here during the experience in a noticeable way. They can heal you, teach you, and reconnect with you when doing this.

You can achieve positive results through meditation, clearing, and setting your intention on helping others and yourself. Everything related to positive change is agreed upon at a higher level and planned out in detail by your Higher Self.

Sometimes the Beings you work with experience going into a crystal chamber. You can also experience the crystal chamber, physically and energetically. These chambers can teleport you, heal you, or be a medium for you to experience whatever is required for your growth.

There are Pleiadian, Sirian, Orion, and many other Star Nation and Elohim-type rock beds that are portals all over the world, galaxy, and beyond. They allow you to connect with whatever you have the level of consciousness to access.

Some of these devices interlock into a network for those with the same intention and vibration. You can visit astrally and bi-locate through these devices. You can also physically manifest in some of the locations these devices are connected to.

Some of these chambers have been used to help those who have committed wrong actions, in order to recalibrate them back to a normal, positive state. In these cases, no incarceration is needed, because the core issues underlying why these individuals have done wrong is repaired from the light blueprint level, which these devices can work on.

Most of the time, bi-locating happens on Earth by the use of these chambers. Most of you bi-locate all the time, which means you are in two or more places at once. However, unless you are tuned into your thoughts and your Third Eye, much will go unnoticed, including your thoughts and any downloads you receive. You will attain *knowledge*, but without knowing how you know it. Some of the Inner Earth Beings and the ancient Lemurians still use these chambers to help people heal and learn. In general, they assist those who ask for help.

Some of you work with energy. You feel, sense, see, and manipulate energy. Some of you move your hands when helping others with their healing. In this way, you are manipulating energy bands and removing blockages, implants, hooks, attachments, agreements, tracking devices, parasitic thought forms, and the like. Some of you also do healing with sound, including tones you make yourself and using crystal bowls. When you perform this service for others, a higher part of you is coming in and anchoring in this realm what you know from other facets of yourself.

Through connecting with you own God self, and the Elohim self, your cell of Source will override all and you will be able to do what any of these devices can do, and much more. Some of you don't know why or how you do what you do, but you just do it and get results. This is why! You are connecting with your Guides or something else wonderful that is working through you. Sometimes, this might mean other Beings you have invited (meaning other people's Guides), which can happen when you are helping others. It can even be your Higher Self or another facet of you assisting, too. You are calibrating the light, the liquid light, the living light, when healing from the light blueprint.

The Angels assist you constantly through the light blueprint. For example, they can divide off a facet of themselves, in any place or vibration and at any time. They are among you and some facets of them have magnetized Light Bodies, which are an orange/golden light color. Some of their Andromedan facets appear like this, in the same way as the Angels you already know about. There are even geometric facets to them and they work on multiple layers. When they manifest in your density and vibration, they might appear as

Rainbow Light Beings or as one of the rainbow spectrums of light.

They calibrate to whatever they connect with for the benefit of both parties. The Brotherhoods, the Councils, and the beautiful many are working with you. The Nature Beings, the ET Beings, and those from the many realms and beyond are with you.

Everything is leading to all of humanity reconnecting with the light vibrations. Rainbows are a reminder of this. Some are manifestations of portals that work on the light blueprint vibration principle.

When many humans see a rainbow, they look at the rainbow as a whole first and then the individual colors. They feel like they are seeing something they know on a deeper level and that there is more to it.

The colors of the light realms are of the highest order, before becoming the rainbow realm, which encompasses all the light realms and leads to the golden plane of bliss, and then to the void, interconnecting with the other Source cells that are part of a greater intelligence.

When you see two rainbows together, and they have colors appearing in the opposite order to each other, you are witnessing a portal opening up on a light blueprint level.

The rainbow is a physical manifestation of this opening. With it can come rain and weather disturbances. These disturbances are manifestations in the physical from the light blueprint when a portal comes into this realm.

Some humans experience something similar to ascension waves when they see double rainbows. This means the Earth is opening up and clearing an acupuncture point in the area of the rainbows.

There are Guardians and original spirits at all of the portals. They are sometimes interlocking from the light blueprint with the Elohim, depending on the circumstances.

Each color of light is a realm, a vibration, and part of the overall ascension process and the higher realms. Some of you might feel you belong to a specific color, a soul group. This means some part of you resonates best with one of the colors that is part of the many light vibrations your oversoul encompasses. When this happens, it means you are reconnecting with whatever resonates with you and is needed at the time.

Many who reconnect with the rainbow plane can ignite their Rainbow Light Body. When this happens, they fly around in their Merkabah assisting on many planes (from the light blueprint level) and teleporting through the electron, as they work with Metatron and the Elohim.

Be open to each experience. See it with your mind's eye and feel the sensations and energies. Be persistent and maintain your balance.

Once your intention is set strong with human emotion (through focus and intent), you will be able to manifest whatever you seek. It's amazing what you can manifest when you are persistent.

Your Guides and Higher Self are working with each and every one of you from the light blueprint in the way you asked them to. On occasion, agreements will change because of how you react and get off-track and other circumstances.

Some want the nuts and bolts of their experiences, while others just want the love and light frequency. The fact is you need a little of both, and more, to understand the mechanics of all this while experiencing it through your human mind.

You might start out linear with your experiences. In time, this will shift to multidimensional awareness, as most of you already know.

Once science (from all backgrounds) recognizes the Brotherhoods who serve the collective consciousness, then much of your fields will take a leap forwards. This will lead to greater understanding about who you are and your reality.

Anything can be accessed once you are open to receiving. It all has to do with setting your intention, being of service to others, and riding the energy. You are already opening up and receiving, although some of you might not understand how or why. But you will—and you will also know you have never been alone.

January 17, 2017
Shi-Ji via Peter Maxwell Slattery

Chapter 8
God's Mind, Your Mind

The coming vibrational change will bring forth change on Earth. Those who are ready will move to their next level. For some, a robe of light will come onto them and slowly they will shed their physical body and become a Being of Light.

For some, it will be a reunion (a cosmic one) connecting them to their ancestors, the Anunnaki, Lyrans, Star Nations, and family from afar and beyond, although the biggest and most powerful reunion will be with Source.

The build-up to this great reunion has begun, and some have already gone. Now, with the balancing of the feminine and masculine energies, the vibration is right for the connection to be made.

Those of you who are ready to evolve can connect to these greater realities and go.

Gaia and the Inner Earth Beings—with assistance from the Star Nations, the Guardians, the Brotherhoods, and the Elohim—are paving the way for this to be done in a way that will not shock the system.

Doing your part and working on yourself is all that needs to be done. Those who would give the shirt off their back to help someone don't need to know what you know. It is not part of their journey, because they are already in service mode.

Those who have more of a job to do for the conscious grid can assist on many levels, through thought and energy. Many don't need to do much more than use their thoughts and energy. This is their job, because it holds space and affects those around them on multiple levels that are unknown to most. Everyone's job is just as important as everyone else's.

Meditation, grounding, clearing your energy bands through practices, eating high vibrational foods (fruit and vegetables mostly), exercise, fun time, alone time, family time, lovers time, relaxing time, and work—all of this needs to come into play in balance and harmony. The shift is on such a grand scale. There are even some species waiting for the next level, but, unfortunately, they are being held back because the shift is being held back due to the actions of the Lower Light.

Many are waiting for change. Some Beings are floating throughout space in huge motherships with entire ecosystems. Some are having adventures and exploring, looking for a place to create a new civilization, although some are in this situation because they have outlived their home world, or worlds. The situations of these Beings are different, but all of them are ready for the next level—although, like you, the Lower Light is affecting them.

Some look to other races and Beings as Gods; they are still learning like everyone else and going through their self-mastery experience. No one is immune to evolution.

Humans are holding back because their thoughts are so powerful. Once humans are open and connected to a higher level of consciousness, the conditions for all will change because of critical mass. Human thoughts have been a great power source for the Artificial Intelligence.

Humans do not know who they are, what they are, what they are capable of, or their royal DNA, the hybrid super-mix they come from. All of these attributes came into being from the other races on the Earth after the program of hybridization (which happened long ago and is continuing). Earth Humans surpass all other multidimensional Beings, but they are unaware of the Lower Light. When they are trapped and focused on fear, greed, sex, and external interests, human energy is a huge power hit (like a drug) for the Lower Light Network.

Each of you, individually and as a collective, has your own book. This book is continually being written on multiple levels, and it is eternal. Your history goes back a long way. Your glyphs tell part of the story, the forgotten tablets of old, and what's still underground in Australia, New Zealand,

Indonesia, America, South America, Antarctica, Siberia, Canada, the Middle East, the Gobi desert, Africa, India, and Russia, and what's under the ocean in multiple areas. All of these represent history going back so far that it's unfathomable to most.

Much of the evidence will never be found because of Earth changes, cataclysms in the past on a huge scale, and because Gaia is evolving and shifting its plates—with assistance from the energies in the cosmos over many billions of years. As a result, much of the evidence has been lost, although most of it can be accessed through your mind, which is God's mind.

Significant change is going to take place, and much has already taken a toll—not just on the Earth Humans, but also the wildlife, the many races of

Bigfoot, fairies, spirits, Guardians, elementals, nature spirits, Orbs, the Inner Earth Beings, Gaia, and more.

Many have watched the chaos for some time. Now there is the possibility of civil and race wars in America and continued unrest in the Middle East. The direction of the world's attention is on Russia, China, and the U.S.A. and its allies. All of this is just a show, because a greater force is in control and directing it.

However, everything can change with a thought. The people and their controllers who contribute to the unrest of the world are feeding the Artificial Intelligence. In the coming days, no one will be able to run from what's about to happen. From the Vatican crumbling to disclosure, change will occur in ways most cannot imagine.

Many things are possible and everything can change in an instant. It all has to do with when and how the energies align. The wars are taking place in the heavens, both in this vibration and beyond. The bloodlines are being affected from the inside out. Now the Lower Light Network will try to push the cyborg and transhumanism agenda (which is already in effect) because it has been used on their pawns (Super Soldiers, etc.) as test subjects. The black goo is part of the virus that will affect the masses on another level.

Some have black box devices with multiple applications. They are being used for free energy, as a portal to other dimensions, as a medium for weaponry and travel, and even for trapping souls. Just like everything else, these devices can be used for good or bad. This is an example of how everything depends on intention and the mind using the means it has access to.

To have access back to the light blueprint and beyond depends on your consciousness. From a higher level of consciousness, murder, rape, and fear cannot exist because the higher vibrations are resonating love.

Just as the Atlantians are in relation to the Nazis and the Secret Space Program, and those behind the scenes manipulating the masses, on the opposite side there are the Lemurians and the Star Nations, who are assisting those in service.

Much is not known about Atlantis. Some say it exploded as the result of scientific experiments, others say from an asteroid. Both are right. Their demise was the result of their level of consciousness. They still exist, but they are hidden, as in, "Out of sight, out of mind."

The Egyptians came to Australia after Atlantis and Lemuria. They considered it to be a teaching place. Over time, they took the knowledge of the Original people for themselves, which resulted in the demise of the two pharaohs who had made the decision. So much is unknown to the masses.

Wars are taking place in your solar system. The good and bad are going at each other, and higher levels of consciousness and forgiveness are very much needed—because unity consciousness does not create division.

Embrace who you are in this experience and beyond. Keep being you. Your individuality and uniqueness are what this is all about. Everyone and every experience must be different.

You are beautiful inside and out. You are capable of anything. Reprogram your body computer with affirmations (if needed), un-brainwash yourself, and do research. Focus on connecting with everything you, your peers, and the masses have been vibrationally blocked from experiencing.

Set aside the ego, because it divides you from others. Get back to your heart center and join in the love that carries with it brotherly and sisterly love, omnipresence, equality, and abundance. This will connect you to the Brotherhoods, your Guides, your other facets and your Higher Self, the Elohim self, and your God self.

You have been given great tests, and you will continue to have them for some time, individually and as a collective. Politically and environmentally there will be more tests and changes. In all areas of your life and in society, welcome the process and rejoice in the coming evolution of humanity. Change is upon you all, and it's up to you what to make of it.

The last of the trumpets is being played. Revelations are upon you, and so is the choice to go where you want. Nothing is impossible. You can do anything because you are the master of your own experience. The veils are lifting. Some of you might see flashes, lightening in your presence, in your homes, and locations around you. These are the Brotherhoods, the Guardians, your Guides, and the Elohim connecting with you through the light blueprint. They are with you all the time through thought.

Freedom can be found in your presence—enjoy it with your friends, family, and others. You can have it anytime. The mind can either be your prison, or it can be your unbounded playground to roam free. You decide.

You are all that is, has been, and ever will be. You are connected to everything. You're an expression of all that is. There is nothing you cannot achieve. Everything starts in the mind: God's mind, your mind.

All that is keeping you from manifesting and doing what you feel in your heart is your limited view and your fear. You can start at anytime, and remember...there is no right or wrong way to go about any of this. Be the master of your experience, this self-mastery experience. Be your own guru and a guide to others, just as they are guiding you in this realm and beyond.

Love is all that matters. Love is the key to everything. The limitations you set are those you set for yourself. Enjoy your life knowing you are a Creator Being deep down inside, and this will shift all energies.

The truth of the matter is that you can do anything, create anything, be anything, experience anything, and manifest anything, but there is a catch: you must have gratitude.

Gratitude is a must, and it must come from the heart, the vibration of the heart. It cannot be pushed or brought on by just thinking it. Gratitude needs to come from the heart. When you are grateful, your heart vibration mixes with the love vibration and the geometry, resulting in changing the game again, moving you up to the next level. Service to others on a larger scale will come with the art of self-mastery.

Compassion, empathy, and being nonjudgmental, and also love and gratitude, can bring forth a multiple geometric overlay, bringing the Elohim light blueprint closer to God's mind, your mind. From there, you can anchor other energies and be a portal for your Guides and the Guides of others.

It all starts with love, unconditional and unbounded love, which connects with unbounded, non-linear minds, connecting you back to the Elohim oversoul cell of Source—a cell of a greater intelligence of which you are part—because everything is in symbiotic relationship.

You are all that is. God's mind and your mind are one and the same. Love, light and bliss, from our hearts to yours.

January 18, 2017
Shi-Ji via Peter Maxwell Slattery Final Note

Final Note

Just like I wrote for the Final Note in *The Book of Shi-Ji*, "Make of this what you may, and interpret this as you may."

Love, light, and bliss,
Peter Maxwell Slattery

The Book of Shi-Ji 2

GLOSSARY

Aboriginal (Original Person – preferred name for Aboriginals) Masters – Ascended Aboriginal or Aboriginal who has obtained spiritual enlightenment and is in service to Earth and Source.

Akashic records – A place, or realm, where all events throughout all planes and dimension are held and knowledge accessible to all.

(the) Archons, the Lower Light – Part of the Elohim that stayed within Source and did not go back to their God state. They are the force stopping all Beings from connecting back to Source; they attempt to control and keep supremacy over all. They are also created an Artificial Intelligence that harvests negative energy; they run on negative energy and feed off negative energy and events from the human race and all beings; this keeps them in existence.

Ascended Master – Spiritually enlightened Beings who obtained enlightenment after many incarnations and are now in service to humanity, the earth, the universe, and Source.

Astral, astral travel – Leaving the body in energy / conscious form and travelling the universe and its planes and dimensions.

Astral mansions – Other dimensions.

Atlantis and Lemuria – Two previous civilizations on Earth that were Pleiadian Colonies.

Bases – A facility that is run, owned, and operated by branches of extraterrestrial groups or races, or by humans or military, as a command center or outpost. Bases shelter crafts and have equipment and research facilities, manage operations, and store supplies.

Being(s), Ancient Beings (spirit beings, but also used here for human beings) – ET Beings, Light Beings, humans, anything that has consciousness.

Being of Light – Conscious Being structured from light.

(other) Beings – Feline Beings, Bird Beings, Mantis Beings, Nordics, and human-looking Beings – humanoid type conscious Beings with traits of an Earth human, but can have different features.

Black Goo – Biological substance, a virus, black, sometimes brown in appearance, which infects a person to control or take over them in order manipulate the person to carry out the agenda of the Lower Light. In effect, can also take out, kill, or make ill any enemy of the Lower Light.

Book of Knowledge – Book that holds knowledge and wisdom in all areas and subject matters.

Brotherhood of Light – Highly evolved spiritual conscious Beings who can assume any form; they are responsible for holding order throughout the universe for Source. They pave the way and also hold space for civilizations to evolve.

(the) Council of the Whole – A Council with the job of regulating all within Source and bringing balance.

(the) Council of Nine – A group of advanced light beings who are teachers and regulators for the evolution of the universe; they assist all councils.

(Orion) Council of Light – A spiritually advanced group of Beings that regulate and assist the Orions and also other races.

Craft(s) – Commonly referred to as UFOs or spacecrafts – Some are structured with exotic materials; others are Light vehicles (Merkabah) structured from consciousness and light. Some are grown and are organic. Crafts are trans-dimensional, able to time travel and breach the speed of light, and can have consciousness themselves.

Crop circles – Geometrical formations found mainly in farmers' fields and crops; they carry messages and information. Mainly done by extraterrestrials on Earth and other advanced civilizations, although some are faked by Earth Humans or military to make the masses think there is nothing to them.

3-D Level – The third density, or dimension, that humans are experiencing at this time.

Disclosure – The discovery of truth or information that has been suppressed.

(the) Elohim (also known as Anunnaki) – The First Beings that manifested on planetary bodies in physical form that were not female or male.

"Anunnaki" also means those who came to Earth from the heavens, as described in ancient Sumerian text; another name for the Original Lyrans that came into being in the Elohim state.

Epigenetics – The study of heritable changes in gene function that do not involve changes in DNA sequence. Storing of past traits of ancestors in your genetics.

Experiencer – Someone who has had or is having experiences of what is deemed to be paranormal experiences or contact with another form of supernatural intelligence (the supernatural and paranormal are actually normal).

Extraterrestrials, E.T.s – Intelligences from elsewhere in the universe and beyond; not from Earth.

Eye of Source/Source's Eye/God's Eye – Awareness of all, the consciousness of Source seeing and experiencing all through everyone's eyes and consciousness.

(the) Fallen Ones – a term from the Bible referring to the Archons (the Lower Light); the Elohim that left source and did not stay in their God state; they manipulate and create negative energy so they can stay and exist.

Fractal – Any of various extremely irregular curves or shapes for which any suitably chosen part is similar in shape to a given larger or smaller part when magnified or reduced to the same size.

Gaia – Another name for Earth.

Gatekeeper – A Being who is responsible for and protector of a dimensional gate, a stargate, or portal, that allows access to and from other places and realms.

(the) Guardians – Those that protect and defend, regulate and monitor all that is.

Guide(s) (spirit guides) – An entity or Being that is not incarnated in a physical body, and that is protecting or guiding humans during the human experience. Sometimes they are extraterrestrial; they can also be other facets of the consciousness of the person who perceives them as a Guide from another realm, or dimension.

Inter-planes – The planes between dimensions and densities; all inter-planes are in the same place, or dimension.

Light Being, Light Cities – Beings with consciousness structured from light or cities structured from light.

Light blueprint – Blueprint of all that exists; made from light that came from Source's awareness.

(the) Lower Light (Network) – See "Archon" for definition.

Merkabah: (Light Vehicle) – Created from an individual Being's light body and consciousness that can be trans-dimensionally travelled in.

Metatron – Worker Being for Source, who is the Master of the Electron, regulating all thought, consciousness, movement, through all planes and dimensions and is everywhere at once through the Electron.

Michael – Worker Being for Source; a protector Being who regulates all that is; works in synch with Metatron and can also be everywhere at once.

Moldavite – By-product of Pleiadian craft that was once shot down and came into Earth's atmosphere. Moldavite is forest green, olive green, or blue/green. Although Pleiadian in origin, the mainstream media says it's a silica projectile rock formed by a meteorite impact in Southern Germany that occurred about 15 million years ago. Also known as a type of tektite.

Morgellons disease – An uncommon, poorly understood condition characterized by small fibers or other particles emerging from skin sores. People with this condition often report feeling as if something is crawling on or stinging their skin.

Nanotechnology – Science, engineering, and technology conducted at the nanoscale level. Nanotechnology is also manipulation of matter on an atomic, molecular, and supramolecular scale.

Nephilim – Hybrid, part ET or otherworldly being, and part human.

New Earth – A new vibrational frequency of Earth; those who have elevated their level of consciousness can start to experience and perceive the New Earth. Some can shift into the frequency; this New Earth is right beside the frequency you are now experiencing.

Orb – Can appear as a ball of light and has consciousness; orbs can be an E.T., spirit, nature spirit, elemental, fairy, bigfoot, and many other types of intelligences. Some appear in their natural form, or they can appear as one, or it can be a by-product before a Being appears in physical form. Also, some are monitoring devices, a drone, or a Merkabah of a Being. An orb is basically an intelligence that is trying to explode from another frequency into your reality.

Oversoul – Your Higher Self, your Elohim self, which is a cell of Source.

Portals – Gateways and transporter to other places, realms.

Remote viewing – Being able to perceive anywhere in space and time, local or non-local or non-linear.

Reptilians – Humanoid beings of many different types and shapes and sizes. They work with the Archons (the Lower Light) to control the human races, although some are seeing their ways and changing due to not being able to evolve in consciousness (because they are in service to self and the lower light).

OTHER HUMANOID BEINGS:

Jinn – Supernatural Beings that are either in self-service mode or they are trickster Beings that are not positive or negative; they can appear in any form if they wish to do so.

Greys – They come in many different colors, but mainly grey; they are the typical aliens people hear about with the big, black, almond-shaped eyes; they are skinny and have big heads. They come from many places; some were once human and some are androids. Some are in service to humanity or other forces; they can be of a positive or negative nature.

Shadow Beings – They appear as shadows in humanoid form; they are mainly in self-service mode or they are working for the Lower Light.

Mantis Beings (Insectoids) – One of the most ancient races in the universe; they are mainly mediators and scientific in nature; they look like mantis' or part humanoid and part mantis; they come in many sizes and colors.

Throne Beings – A type of Light Being that resides next to Source.

STARS AND CONSTELLATIONS:

Sirius – Binary star system.

Pleiades – Star Cluster.

Orion – Star Constellation.

Alnilam – A star in Orion's Belt.

Arcturus – Giant red star located in the constellation Boötes.

Lyra – A relatively small constellation.

Alnitak – One of the three stars in Orion's Belt.

Andromeda – A constellation and also there is the Andromeda galaxy.

Merope, Electra – Stars in the Pleiades.

Draco constellation – A constellation in the far northern sky.

Hyades – Star cluster located in Taurus constellation.

Aldebaran – Brightest star in the constellation Taurus.

Melona/Maldek – Now the asteroid belt in your local solar system.

Mars – Planet.

Sirians, Orions, Pleiadians/Plejarens – Beings from Sirius, Orion, and Pleiades that come in many different forms, shapes, sizes, and colors.

Star Family (star traits) – Family you have had past experiences with, or from where you have once incarnated (although all lives are being experienced at the same time).

Starseed – Someone who has lived in other ET civilizations.

Star Nations Galactic Councils, Federation – Names for the collective groups of ET races that are at unity but still respect each other's ways, basically an ET United Nations. They exist to uphold order and balance between the ET races.

(the) Temple – The human body.

Third Eye – Energy center in the human energy body, associated with the pineal gland, which is located basically in the middle of the human brain. It is an antenna and receiver for visuals, and can also can be used to communicate through visuals to anywhere in space and time with other intelligences.

Transhumanism – Human race connected to or having a symbiotic connection technology or individual consciousness connected to or inside a device / robot, allowing the individual to have a synthetic reality.

Twin-Flame – Someone who resonates with you, can be a mirror, is a good balance, can bring balance, and is part of your soul family, which means you have had many missions together and come from the same oversoul, and in some cases, race and soul groups.

UFO – An unidentified flying object.

Walk-in – Another consciousness that can jump into the physical vessel: e.g. the human body, while the original consciousness that was in the body leaves.

The Book of Shi-Ji 2

Books by Peter Maxwell Slattery

The Book of Shi-Ji

The Book of Shi-Ji 2

The Book of Shi-Ji 3

ABOUT THE AUTHOR

Peter Maxwell Slattery is an international bestselling author who is known as an ET contact experiencer. His ET experiences started at an early age and continue to this day, with hundreds of witnesses to events. He has an overwhelming amount of photographic and video evidence related to UFOs, otherworldly Beings, and apparitions, plus physical trace evidence.

His experiences with extraterrestrials have led him to help people and groups make ET contact themselves, in addition to healing and tapping into their own abilities. Pete has appeared on Channel 7's *Prime News* and *Sunrise*, and many other international television programs. He has made worldwide news, been in numerous documentaries, been written about in magazines, and been a guest on mainstream radio shows, including *Coast-to-Coast*. He is also a musician and, as a filmmaker, he has made a number of documentaries on the subject of E.T.s.

Peter Maxwell Slattery continues to open the world up to the greater reality that "We are not alone" and that "We are all amazing, powerful Beings."

For more information go to petermaxwellslattery.com.

Follow Pete on Facebook, YouTube Instagram, and Twitter.

Made in the USA
Columbia, SC
08 May 2019